GREAT MOMENTS IN AMERICAN HISTORY

The Making of the American Flag

Betsy Ross and George Washington

Janet Palazzo-Craig

rosen central
Primary Source™

The Rosen Publishing Group, Inc., New York

Published in 2004 by The Rosen Publishing Group, Inc.
29 East 21st Street, New York, NY 10010

Editors: Jennifer Silate and Geeta Sobha
Book Design: Michael DeLisio
Photo Researcher: Rebecca Anguin-Cohen

Photo Credits: Cover (left), title page, pp. 6, 14 © Bettman/Corbis; cover (right) illustration
© Debra Wainwright/The Rosen Publishing Group; p. 10 Independence National Historical
Park; p. 18 © Getty Images; p. 22 Library of Congress Rare Book and Special Collections
Division; p. 29 Courtesy of The Huntington Library, San Marino, CA; p. 30 Library of
Congress Prints and Photograph Division; p. 31 The Wetherill Family and the Religious Society
of Free Quakers, Photograph courtesy of Independence National Historical Park; p. 32 Maura
B. McConnell, courtesy Betsy Ross House

First Edition

Library of Congress Cataloging-in-Publication Data

Palazzo-Craig, Janet.
    The making of the American flag : Betsy Ross and George Washington /
    Janet Palazzo-Craig.— 1st ed.
        p. cm. — (Great moments in American history)
    Summary: In 1827, Betsy Ross remembers the day in 1776 when George
    Washington came to her upholstery shop to ask for help with designing
    and making an American flag.
    ISBN 0-8239-4335-6 (library binding)
    1. Ross, Betsy, 1752-1836—Juvenile fiction. 2. United
    States—History—Revolution, 1775-1783—Juvenile fiction. [1. Ross,
    Betsy, 1752-1836—Fiction. 2. Flags—United States—Fiction. 3. United
    States—History—Revolution, 1775-1783—Fiction. 4. Washington, George,
    1732-1799—Fiction.] I. Title. II. Series.

PZ7.P1762Mak 2004
[Fic]—dc21

                                                                    2003007274

Manufactured in the United States of America

CONTENTS

Preface

The American Revolutionary War was fought between 1775 and 1783. The fight for independence took place because American colonists were not happy under British rule. The colonists believed they were being unfairly taxed. They also thought they did not have a say in how the government was run.

The war's first fighting took place in Massachusetts on April 19, 1775. It was called the Battle of Lexington and Concord. Shortly after the battle, General George Washington formed the Continental army to fight the British. The colonists who believed that the Americans should be free from British rule were called patriots. One such colonist was Betsy Ross. She and her husband John ran an upholstery shop in Philadelphia, Pennsylvania. In their shop, they sewed clothes, curtains, and other things for the people of Philadelphia.

The Rosses strongly supported the colonists' fight for freedom. John Ross joined the Philadelphia militia. A militia is an army made up of ordinary citizens. In December 1775, John was hurt when the ammunition he was guarding blew up. Betsy nursed his wounds, but John was hurt too badly. He died on January 21, 1776.

After John's death, Betsy, now twenty-four years old, ran the upholstery shop by herself. This was very unusual in colonial times. Women did not often own businesses. Despite this, Betsy made the business a success.

Betsy Ross's life is filled with stories of success in the face of unbeatable odds. Betsy Ross often told her children and grandchildren about her life. One story that Betsy loved to tell them was when George Washington visited her shop. That day, she had no idea what a big role she would come to play in the history of her young nation....

Before the first Stars and Stripes flag was made, colonists used many different flags to represent the American colonies. Betsy Ross had sewn some of these early flags.

Chapter One

A SPECIAL VISIT

*I*t was a bright spring day in Philadelphia in 1827. Sunlight shone through the window of the upholstery shop on Arch Street. Inside, Betsy Ross, now seventy-five years old, sat sewing. Betsy looked out the window. The sunny morning reminded her of a day long ago. Thoughts of Betsy's youth filled her mind. As she looked about the shop, Betsy thought of the days just after her husband John's death. It was the time of the American Revolutionary War. Betsy had seen and done much during that time. Her proudest moment, though, came on a June day in 1776. Betsy remembered it well. It began with a knock at the door of her upholstery shop....

Knock, knock! Betsy looked up from her sewing. *Who could be at the door?* she thought. As she opened the door to the shop, Betsy's eyes widened

7

with surprise. Three men stood before her. The first was General George Washington, the leader of the Continental army. With him were her late husband's uncle, George Ross, and another man she had not met before.

"Good morning, Betsy," said General Washington, smiling at her.

"Good morning, General Washington," answered Betsy. "It is an honor to see you." Betsy knew the general. They had attended church together in Philadelphia. Washington had also hired Betsy and her husband to sew shirts for him. She had not seen the general lately, though. Leading the army during wartime had kept him on the move.

"I believe you know Mr. Ross. And please meet Robert Morris," said General Washington.

"How nice to see you, Uncle," Betsy said to Mr. Ross. "And it is a pleasure to meet you, Mr. Morris. I have heard about how you are raising money for our army."

"Yes," said Mr. Morris. "It is a big job. Our soldiers need food and supplies." Then he added, "We are very sorry to hear of your husband's death."

"He gave his life to help our new nation," added General Washington.

Betsy nodded sadly. "Yes," she said. "I am proud of John and his work for the militia. Now he is gone. It is not easy running the shop on my own. The war has made it very hard to get supplies for my work. Also, business is very slow. These days, people do not have extra money to spend on the things I sew. I hope these hard times will soon be over."

"That is our goal," said General Washington. "First, we must unite all the colonists in our cause. Then I know we will succeed."

"I agree," said Betsy. "But before we talk any more, would you like something to eat?"

"Yes, please," said General Washington.

Betsy hurried to get food for the men. All the while, her head buzzed with excitement. What could be the reason for this special visit?

George Washington became leader of the Continental army in 1775, at age forty-three. After the American Revolutionary War ended in 1781, he became a farmer and trader. He became the first president of the United States in 1789.

Chapter Two

AN IMPORTANT ASSIGNMENT

When Betsy returned with the food, Washington began. "I am sure you are wondering why we have come here today," he said.

"Yes, I am," said Betsy. "I don't think you are here to have more shirts made!"

"You are right about that," answered Washington, laughing. Then he became very serious. "Mr. Morris, Mr. Ross, and I have come to ask for your help."

"We are part of a committee," said Mr. Morris. "It is our job to make a flag for our new nation."

"It will be a new and different flag, for our new nation" added Mr. Ross.

"And it will be the symbol of our new country," said General Washington. "Will you help us, Betsy?"

Betsy's cheeks turned bright pink. She could hardly believe she was being asked to help with such an important task.

"How may I be of help?" she asked.

"General Washington has told us of your great skill as a seamstress," said Mr. Ross.

Betsy blushed again at this praise. She was glad, though, that her hard work was well liked.

"We have also learned that you have already sewn some flags," said Mr. Morris. "That is part of the reason we thought of you."

Betsy nodded.

"We also chose you for another reason," Washington said. "We know you strongly support our struggle for freedom. To win this war we must unite our soldiers. We also must unite all the citizens of the colonies. A new flag will help us do that. Our flag will tell all who see it that we are a new nation. It will also tell the British that we are united in our cause."

"Tell Betsy about our old flag, General Washington," said Mr. Ross.

"Yes, of course," said Washington. "The flag our army uses now is called the Grand Union. We flew it during our battles these past months. But the Grand Union flag has caused us a lot of trouble. It has red and white stripes. In the upper left corner, it has a small red cross and a small white cross. As you know, that makes it look like the British flag, which is called the Union Jack.

"When we fought the British in Boston, our enemies became confused. When we waved our flag, they thought we were waving the British flag. They thought we wanted to give up. It became very clear to me that we need a new flag. So what is your answer, Betsy? Will you help us?"

"I do not know if I can," said Betsy. "But I know I will try."

"Very good then. Let us begin," said Mr. Ross, eagerly.

Betsy Ross often told her children and grandchildren of how she and George Washington worked closely together on the flag.

Chapter Three

THE FLAG TAKES SHAPE

General Washington looked straight into Betsy's eyes. "We are grateful for your help," he said. "First, we would like you to help us design the flag."

Betsy was excited. "Let's start at the beginning," she said. "What are your ideas so far?"

Washington took a drawing out of his pocket. "Here is what we have," he said. He spread the sheet of paper on the sewing table in front of Betsy.

Betsy studied the paper. It showed a square-shaped flag with red and white stripes and thirteen six-pointed stars on a dark-blue background. Right away, Betsy had several ideas. "My first suggestion is to change the shape of the flag," she said. "I have made many flags. They are usually rectangles. Very few are the square shape shown here."

Taking a fresh sheet of paper, Washington drew the shape Betsy described. Then Betsy said, "I like the red and white stripes. They are bold, just like the American colonists. I also like the blue rectangle in the corner. The white stars will look very good on it. I do think, though, that the stars are too scattered. Perhaps if we put them in a special shape, the flag will look better. I see you have thirteen stars. Do they each stand for a colony?"

"Yes," Washington replied. "We thought that there would be thirteen stripes and thirteen stars to stand for the thirteen colonies."

"Perhaps it would be nice to put the stars in a circle. The circle will show that the colonies are united. Together, they make one country," Betsy said, looking at the three men. Each man nodded his approval. They watched as Washington drew the stars on the sketch.

"Your idea makes sense. I think the patriots will like this flag," Washington said with a smile. Mr. Ross and Mr. Morris agreed.

16

"I do have one other idea," Betsy said.

"I think five-pointed stars should be used," she said. "They are very easy to cut out. Watch." Betsy took out a piece of paper. She folded it quickly and neatly. Then she made one easy cut with her scissors. When she unfolded the paper, she held a perfect five-pointed star. The men liked the crisp look of the star.

"Betsy," said Mr. Morris, "it is clear you have many fine ideas. We will talk them over. Will you go to the shipping store by the dock to meet Mr. Rother at this time next week? He will pass you a message from us."

"Yes, I will," replied Betsy.

With that, General Washington took the new sketch and the one he had brought with him. He tucked them into his pocket and bowed. "Thank you again, Betsy," he said. Then the men left.

Betsy sat alone in the shop once again. *What will happen next?* she thought. *Will my design be picked for the new nation's flag?*

This painting, made in 1877, shows Betsy Ross and her assistants sewing the first American flag.

18

Chapter Four

THE MAKING OF
THE FLAG

T he day of the appointment had finally arrived. Betsy hurried along the dock toward the store where she was to meet Mr. Rother.

On entering the store, she saw a man behind the counter. "Good afternoon, sir. Are you Mr. Rother?" she asked.

"Yes, I am. You must be Mrs. Ross. I have an envelope here for you," Rother replied. "Here you go, ma'am," he said as he handed it to Betsy.

"Thank you," said Betsy. She took the envelope. Betsy was excited. She opened it and took out the letter inside. She took a deep breath and started to read. Betsy's eyes opened wide. The letter had wonderful news! Betsy's design had been chosen as one of the final designs for the new flag. She was to sew the flag she had helped design. It was needed

as soon as possible. The letter said that in time, the flag might even become the official flag of the nation. Inside the envelope, there was also a painting of the design she had helped make.

"Thank you, Mr. Rother. Have a good day," Betsy said as she turned to leave the shop.

Betsy got to work right away. For the next week or so, she worked very hard. She measured and cut the cloth for the stripes. There would be six white stripes and seven red stripes. In the upper left-hand corner, she placed the dark-blue rectangle. She carefully sewed the thirteen white stars onto the dark-blue fabric.

At last, the flag was ready. Betsy proudly looked at her work. "Now our country has a star-spangled banner," she told herself. She hoped the committee would agree. She immediately took the flag to Mr. Ross.

The next morning, there was a knock at her door. "Good morning, Betsy," Mr. Ross said when Betsy opened the door. "I have some wonderful news for you. The flag you made for

us was chosen to lead our country in battle. The committee also wanted me to give you an order to make more flags."

Betsy smiled brightly. "How many flags would you like, Uncle?" she asked.

"As many as you can sew. The order is for an unlimited number of flags," Mr. Ross said.

"Oh, thank you! I will get right to work," Betsy said.

"You are quite welcome. I'm sorry but I must go. I'll be back with money for you so that you can buy what you need to get started on the flags," Mr. Ross said as he walked out the door.

One year later, on June 14, 1777, the leaders of the revolution held a meeting. It was called the Second Continental Congress. At the meeting, Congress made Betsy's flag the official flag of the nation.

For a while, things were going well for Betsy and her business. Little did she know, that would soon change. Trouble was coming that would affect everyone.

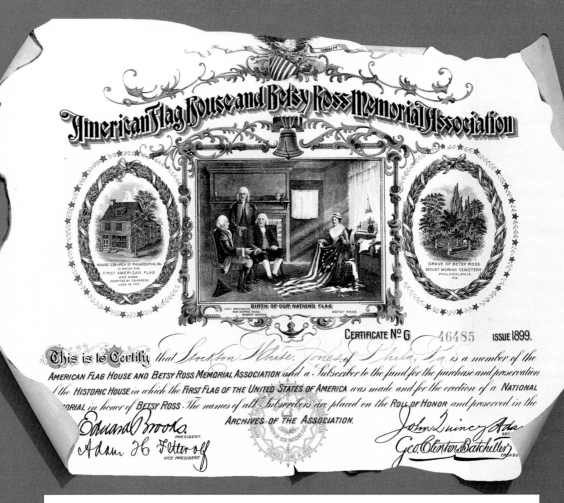

In 1899, the American Flag House and Betsy Ross Memorial Association raised money to help build a memorial to honor Betsy Ross. Each person who gave at least a dime received a certificate like the one shown here. The drawing on the left is Ross's house where the first flag was made. The drawing on the right is of Ross's grave in Philadelphia.

Chapter Five

An End to War

I n the summer of 1777, the Continental army lost several battles. The British took over Philadelphia. Many people fled. Betsy was not one of them. She stayed to make sure her home and her business were safe. Betsy was also worried about her second husband, Joseph Ashburn. The two had married earlier in the year. Joseph was at sea, doing his part to help the colonies. Betsy did not know if he was safe.

The people of Philadelphia faced a very hard winter. British soldiers lived in their houses and ate their food. The soldiers took their valuables, and burned their wooden furniture for firewood. Betsy was frightened, but she stayed brave.

Finally, in the spring of 1778, the British left Philadelphia. They moved toward New York.

Her husband returned from sea for a short time. Their first daughter was born in 1779. In 1780, Joseph left again before their second daughter was born.

In 1781, the Continental army won the war. The people in Philadelphia celebrated. Betsy proudly looked on as flags like the one she had made flew high all over the city.

Betsy was happy, but her happiness was not complete. She had not heard from Joseph or anyone else on his ship. One day, John Claypoole, an old friend, visited Betsy. "Betsy," said John, "I have bad news. During the war, your husband and I were captured. We were kept in the Old Mill." The Old Mill was a British prison in England. It was known for its terrible living conditions.

John looked at Betsy. "I am sorry," he told her. "Joseph died in prison."

Betsy was very sad. She again faced many hard choices. She was now a mother of two little girls. Could she make it on her own? Betsy thought long about it. She decided to try to

keep her shop. She had faced hard times before. She believed she could face this, too.

In time, things got better for Betsy. She kept very busy making flags. Then Betsy found happiness with John Claypoole. They were married in 1783. They ran the upholstery shop together for a long time. They had five daughters, and the family was a happy one.

Betsy's life had not always been easy. Yet her strength and independent spirit had helped her face the hard times. . . .

Knock, knock! Betsy's thoughts about the past would have to wait. Someone was at the door. The old woman went to see who it was. There stood her daughter Clarissa and her niece Margaret Boggs.

"Mother," said Clarissa, "we are here to help you with your work today." The two women had become skilled upholsterers, too.

"What a nice surprise! That is just what I needed," said Betsy. "I have a surprise for you, too. I have decided to stop working as an upholsterer

very soon. I want to give the shop to the two of you. Would you like that?"

"Yes, Mother," said Clarissa. "But what will you do?"

"Do not worry," replied Betsy. "I have been busy for many years. Now, I will rest a bit."

"This is exciting news!" said Margaret. "But we will miss you, Aunt Betsy."

"Yes," agreed Clarissa. "We will miss your good company and your good work. But most of all, we will miss your wonderful stories about your time during the Revolutionary War."

"Those were exciting times," said Betsy. "Often they were trying, but it was worth it all. I am proud to say I helped my country the best way I could. I want you both to promise me that you will keep the story of my visit with General Washington alive."

"We will," said Clarissa. "We will make sure no one ever forgets how you came to make our nation's first star-spangled banner."

Glossary

ammunition (am-yuh-NISH-uhn) things that can be fired from weapons, such as bullets or arrows

colonist (KOL-uh-nist) a person who lives in a newly settled area

committee (kuh-MIT-ee) a group of people chosen to discuss things and make decisions for a larger group

design (di-ZINE) to draw something that can be built or made; the shape or style of something

independence (in-di-PEN-duhnss) freedom

militia (muh-LISH-uh) a group of citizens who are trained to fight but who only serve in times of emergency

patriot (PAY-tree-uht) someone who loves his or her country and is prepared to fight for it

seamstress (SEEM-struhss) a woman who sews for a living

unite (yoo-NITE) to bring people, places, or things together in order to achieve something

upholstery shop (uhp-HOHL-stur-ee SHOP) a store where clothes, curtains, chairs, and other things are sewn

PRIMARY SOURCES

To learn about history, we analyze materials such as photographs, letters, paintings, maps, and even tools of the past. These materials can answer our questions about events that happened long ago.

One such question is whether or not Betsy Ross in fact made the first American flag. As we evaluate the materials left behind by Ross and those who knew her, we can see that there is evidence that she was the maker of the flag. The document shown on page 29 supports the idea that Ross was involved in making the flag.

Many times, items of the past can tell us about the work people did. The tools shown page 32 are from the time Ross worked as an upholsterer. They are examples of tools that she would have used to do her upholstery work. The tools can help us understand how she did her work.

Analysis of historical items such as the document and the tools teach us about important historical events and how people of the past lived.

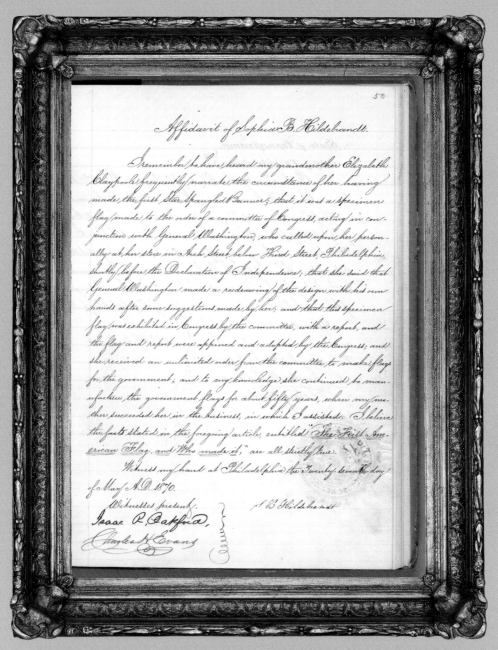

Affidavit of Sophia B. Hildebrandt.

I remember to have heard my grandmother Elizabeth Claypoole frequently narrate the circumstance of her having made the first Star Spangled Banner; that it was a specimen flag made to the order of a committee of Congress, acting in conjunction with General Washington, who called upon her personally at her store in Arch Street below Third Street, Philadelphia, shortly before the Declaration of Independence; that she said that General Washington made a redrawing of the design with his own hands after some suggestions made by her; and that this specimen flag was exhibited in Congress by the committee, with a report, and the flag and report were approved and adopted by the Congress; and she received an unlimited order from the committee, to make flags for the government; and to my knowledge she continued to manufacture the government flags for about fifty years, when my mother succeeded her in the business, in which I assisted. I believe the facts stated in the foregoing article, entitled "The First American Flag, and Who made it," are all strictly true.

Witness my hand at Philadelphia the Twenty-seventh day of May A.D. 1870.

Witnesses present.

Isaac R. Oakford,

Charles H. Evans

S B Hildebrandt

This document dated May 27, 1870, is written by members of Betsy Ross's family. In the document, the writers say that they were often told by Betsy Ross the story of the making of the flag.

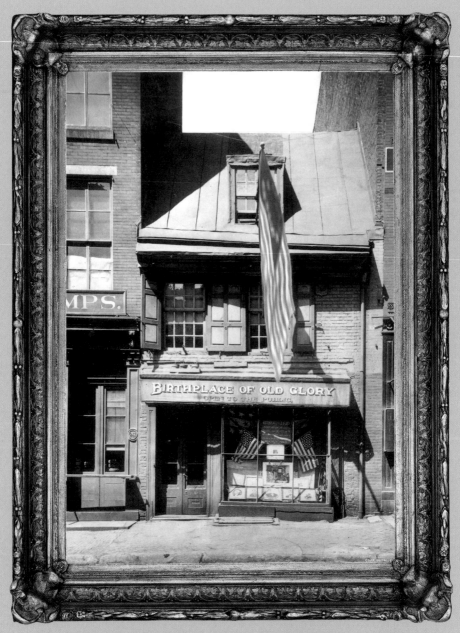

This photograph of Betsy Ross's house was taken about 1900.
The house is now a museum that people can visit.

It is believed that after the flag committee left Betsy's house, Samuel Wetherill, a friend, dropped by to visit. When he heard Betsy's story, he asked to keep the five-pointed star she made for the flag.

These tools are from the Betsy Ross House museum. They are the types of tools that would have been used by upholsterers such as Betsy Ross.